How to Sell on Etsy With Blogging

Selling on Etsy Made Ridiculously Easy Vol.3

by Charles Huff
Founder, Craft Biz Insider

Published in USA by: Craft Biz Insider

Charles Huff

© Copyright 2018

ISBN-13: 978-1-970119-21-3
ISBN-10: 1-970119-21-7

Table of Contents

Also By Charles Huff

About the Author

Charles Huff is a former cubicle drone turned full-time Etsy seller.

He is also the owner of the world's most neurotic Jack Russell Terrier.

A Special FREE Gift for You!

If you'd like FREE instant access to my special report "Top 10 Marketing Tools Every Etsy Seller Should Use" then head over to **CraftBizInsider.com/Free**.

(What else you gonna do? Watch another "Twilight" movie?!)

Prologue: Yeah, But How Do You Make Money With a Blog?

"Do one thing every day that scares you."

-Eleanor Roosevelt

You're skeptical. I get that.

Everyone and their 72-year-old grandma have a blog these days. And very few of those blog owners make a single penny from it.

In fact, a recent study found that nearly 90% of all blog owners in the U.S. make LESS than $100 a year from their blogs.

Not a month. But a year. Not exactly the most impressive ROI (Return on Investment) imaginable.

So, I can understand if you're gun-shy about spending a ton of time and resources on blogging, when every human on the planet seems to have three blogs, and making money with blogs is getting HARDER, not easier. (More on that later.)

I can understand if you ALREADY have a blog but have seen little in the way in terms of traffic or added sales, why you'd want to focus your energies elsewhere.

I can ALSO understand why you'd question the necessity of a blog when you've already got OTHER platforms to worry about such as:

- Your Etsy store
- Your Facebook Fan Page
- Your Pinterest Profile
- Your Twitter Account
- Your email newsletter
- Whatever else you have on your to-do list

But here's the thing, and if you've read my other books in this series you know I think social media is a vital part of the Etsy seller's overall marketing plan…

Blogs kick serious butt because:

- **You own the real estate.** Unlike social media platforms, such as Facebook, and your Etsy store which are rented land.

- **Google and the rest of the search engines LOVE blogs** — way more than static websites.

- **It's a lot easier to capture a lead** (such as an email address) on your blog.

- **It's a lot easier to showcase your products** on your blog (such as a sale or discount).

- **There are ton of cool themes** to make your blog look super professional (most of them for under $40)

- **There are tons of cool plugins** to encourage sharing, boost leads, customize checkout pages, create up-sell pages…and overall make more money!

And though I don't think any of us are in this just for the money — we would have become a stockbroker or a Kardashian for that — I do believe that having a sustainable business that makes an ACTUAL living doing something you love is ONE of the best ways to serve the world.

"You Like Me! You Really, Really Like Me!"

Ten years ago, the things I'm going to show you how to do would have taken thousands of dollars and a master's degree in Computer Science.

Now, for less than the cost of an Amazon Kindle you can have a fully-customized Etsy seller blog that showcases your personality and products — with built-in automation to help you make money while you sleep.

I don't know about you, but I love to make

money while I'm sleeping.

So, if you're ready, let's hit the snooze button and begin your journey toward becoming an Etsy business blogging master!

Chapter 1:
Building the Perfect Blog in Six (Mostly) Easy Steps

"The greatest enemy of a good plan is the dream of a perfect plan."

-Carl von Clausewitz

My 73-year-old mom set up her OWN blog. By herself.

That should tell you everything you need to know about the "difficulty" of setting up a blog.

This doesn't mean it's not a bit technical. Web developers love to use vague, esoteric terms — such as wireframes and 301 redirects —when something simpler would suffice.

But here's the awesome, cool thing about setting up a blog:

Whatever you don't know HOW to do, or don't WANT to do, somebody else will do FOR you.

Cheap.

- **Don't know how to design a header for your blog?** A kick-butt graphic designer can crank that out in 24 hours.

- **Don't know how to install a WordPress plugin or even know which plug-ins you need or what the heck a WordPress plug-in actually does?** A virtual assistant (VA) can pull that off in under five minutes.

- **Not sure how to FTP your files…or even what the heck FTP stands for?** Your average tormented fourteen-year-old will do it in exchange for a burrito. (Extra guacamole.)

As we go over the FIVE Essential Steps for Blog Set-Up in this chapter, remember if something seems super confusing or overly technical, take a breath.

Relax.

And realize you **don't need to know** every little aspect of blog publishing.

You just need to know enough to make a quick decision. (And then delegate it to somebody who DOES know what the heck they're doing.)

And don't worry, I'll give you some great resources I use to find freelancers who, for just a couple of dollars, will handle all the stress for you.

So, let's get started with…

Step No.1: Pick a Lane

There are essentially four different website lanes to choose from:

- You pay a web developer/designer to create your site from scratch for $1500+

- You use a 100% FREE option, such as Typepad or Blogger

- You pay a moderate monthly fee ($15-$25) to a company like Wix or SquareSpace and let them do all the heavy-lifting

- You pay a moderate one-time fee ($50-$75) and build your site on the FREE WordPress platform

Of the above options I don't recommend the first TWO.

Having a custom-built website is not only expensive, and requires that you know exactly what you want, but it also necessitates constant upkeep. (To-tal pain.)

And the 100% FREE options, such as Typepad

and Blogger, just don't give you enough flexibility to whip your website into Etsy-selling shape.

The last two are good options. It all depends on what you want and how comfortable you are with the tech.

If the phrase HTML conjures nightmares from which you know you'll never awake, and you don't have a clue what your website should look like, then build your blog/website with Wix or SquareSpace.

Of the two Wix is the more simple and easier to use. But SquareSpace offers interesting functionalities you can't get with Wix.

But if you have a fair inkling of what you want your website/blog to look like, or you plan to create quite a bit of content, you'll probably want to go the WordPress route.

If that's the case, here's what you'll need to get started:

A registered domain (more on this in next chapter) $10/yr.

Web hosting (somewhere to park your website) - HostGator (CraftBizInsider.com/hostgator) is one of the cheapest and best in the business.

A WordPress theme (something to make your website pretty) - I like these two themes: Gather (From ThemeTrust) and Elite (From ThemeForest)
Somebody to install all this stuff for you (More on that later)

Action Step: *Choose a "lane" for your website needs. Wix and SquareSpace are good if you don't want to deal with the tech. WordPress, with the Gather or Elite theme, are good if you have a clear aesthetic in mind.*

Step No.2: Pick a Schnazzy Website Domain Name

Your website domain is just a fancy word for the website URL, or web address, where your blog will live. (Example: http://YourCoolDomain.com.)

Years ago there was real benefit to stuffing your domain with a keyword-friendly phrase, such as...

CuteDecorativeJustinBieberCandleHolders.com

But the Google police have since cracked down at such blatant attempts to game the search engine results. (Thankfully.)

These days it's a much better idea to either go with:

- A domain centered around your Etsy store name
- Or a branded personality name, such as SuzyCreations.com

Choosing a domain name is a very personal thing, so I wouldn't want to tell you what you HAVE to do, but here are a couple of things to keep in mind:

- **Keep your domain short**. Skip the long verbal flourishes and complicated names.

- **Avoid any words that could, or are often, misspelled.** My mom once had a blog called "PotpourriChronicles.com." You have no idea how many different ways people "try" to spell "potpourri." Save yourself the anguish and keep it simple.

- **Choose a domain that looks good on a business card.** This will be the blog name you'll be sharing with people at trade shows and on every one of your social media properties. Make sure it's something you feel comfortable with.

- **Try to use the .com extension, whenever possible.** .Org extensions are okay, but not as ideal as the .com extension. (Whatever you do, stay away from the .biz or .net. Those come off as very spammy.)

"I've Got a Name"

So once you've got a possible domain name, how do you make sure you own it?

Well, if you're going with Wix or SquareSpace they SHOULD take care of this for you.

But if you're going the WordPress route, it's a simple 2-step process:

- **Head over to a domain registration company and create a profile**. My domain registrar of choice is Namecheap, but you could use any number of them. (Just Google "domain registration" and you'll find hundreds of them.)

- **Do a search to make sure your desired domain isn't already taken**. If it is, you may have to get a little creative with your domain name.

- **If it's available, buy it…now!** Don't wait. The good domains tend to get snagged pretty darn quickly.

Sometimes, if the domain name you like is taken, you'll see contact info that will let you reach out to the domain owner for possible purchase of the domain. I would avoid this like the plague.

People who "squat" on domains tend to want hundreds, if not thousands, of dollars for their domain. No matter how awesome the domain is, it just won't be worth it.

Whatever domain registrar you go with, be sure to avoid GoDaddy. They're miserable to deal with.

Action Step: *Come up with a great domain name…then go buy it at a domain registration company, such as Namecheap.*

Step No.3: Assemble Your Team and Build Your Blog

So, by this point you're probably pulling your hair out, freaking out over the fact that it all sounds about as easy as building a cold-fusion laser in your basement.

Relax. It's super simple, especially when you pay somebody a couple of bucks to install the blog for you.

Now, if you and I were in the good old Internet Marketing biz, I would suggest you learn every in and out of building a blog. But you know what…we're in the artisan craft business….not in the "Hey, click on this shiny ad" business.

So, here's what I suggest you do:

- **Head over to a site like Upwork** and create a job posting titled "WordPress Blog Installation." I've created a sample job posting template over at CraftBizInsider.com/WordPress job that you can grab and use for reference. (This will make sure you get everything done you need.)

- **Choose the 4-5 best candidates and ask them to send references and samples of their work**. Be sure to note how quickly they get back to and if their references seem genuine.

- **Interview the one or two best candidates over Skype**. Try to avoid simply sending email questions. Ask them about their best experiences and their worst. And make sure they document everything.

- **Choose the winning candidate** and wait for your blog to be created.

I usually pay anywhere from $75-$100 for this service. You need plug-ins to sync up with your Etsy store, so it can be a bit complicated, but for the two or three hours it saves me that is totally worth it.

Action Step: *Head over to Upwork and find a freelancer to handle all your blog creation needs.*

Step No.4: Learn the Least You Need to Know About WordPress Blogs

I've tried to keep the technical stuff to a bare minimum in this chapter. (I know us Etsians weren't put on this earth to learn FTP settings and pixel sizes.)

But, when your blog is up and running, you will NEED to know how to create blog posts and pages and name your categories as you build out your blog/website.

If you're gonna use Wix, here's an easy tutorial walking you through the process: CraftBizInsider.com/Wix101.

If you're gonna use SquareSpace, here's video showing you how it's done:

CraftBizInsider.com/Square101

But if you're gonna go the WordPress route, then you'll need a bit more schooling.

And while I could I spend the next four paragraphs writing explaining how to publish on WordPress — I think you gotta see it to really understand it.

So, I've included a really cool beginner guide video from my friend Robert on how to start posting on your WordPress blog. You can see it over at CraftBizInsider.com/WordPress.

Don't worry. Within 15 minutes you'll know everything you need to know about WordPress blogging. (And you'll be that much closer to creating an Etsy sales generating machine.)

Action Step: *Watch my friend Robert's video over at CraftBizInsider.com/WordPress to get the straight scoop on posting on WordPress. Otherwise, if you're gonna use Wix or SquareSpace, then just check out their tutorial videos.*

Chapter 1 Key Takeaways:

- **Though I will not force you, I highly recommend you EITHER** use a company like Wix or SquareSpace for your website or host your own site on the WordPress platform.

- **When choosing a domain name for your blog,** always go for branding over keywords. If you do find your targeted name is available, grab it. Immediately!

- **Have a freelancer at a site like Upwork to install your WordPress blog for you.** Should cost you no more than $100. Well worth it.

- **Spend 15 minutes or so learning the ins and outs of posting on your website platform of choice.** It's easy and will make your life much easier if you take the time to learn it now.

Chapter 2:
How to Turn Your Blog Into a Cash Machine

"Marketing is too important to be left to the marketing department."

-David Packard

Congratulations! You've done most of the hard work. (Or paid somebody to do it for you.)

Before we jump into the deep end of the blogging pool there are just a couple of additional tweaks we need to do to your blog to ensure it does the most important thing of all: make you some money.

None of the stuff I mention below is terribly difficult to implement — most of the time involves you uploading a zip file to your blog. Which you can easily get your VA (Virtual Assistant) to handle for you.

It's important you add all the goodies mentioned in this chapter to your blog strategy, because these ninja hacks (as my Internet marketing cousin likes to call 'em) help make it easy for visitors to spread the word about your products — and even easier to buy your stuff directly from your blog.

So let's get right into it with…

Blog Hack No.1: Put Your Etsy Store on Your Blog

The great thing about a WordPress blog is that there are so many free/cheap plugins that will do amazing things like:

- Let you embed your products on specific pages or posts.

- Allow you to create visually-rich galleries of your store items.

- Give you the flexibility to customize the look and feel of your "mini" Etsy store.

- Help make it easy to inter-link your various products and blog posts in a seamless and easy way.

When it comes to free WordPress plugins that allow us to feed our Etsy store offerings directly onto our blog there are really two options:

- Etsy Shop WordPress Plugin - This plugin allows you to use short codes — simple bits of semantic text — to embed your products in WordPress pages or posts. It doesn't have a ton of extra features, but for a nice basic Etsy store plugin — that won't overwhelm you with choices — this one is a good way to go.

- Etsy Treasure Posting Tool Plugin - I'm shocked that this is a free plugin, considering how much it can really do. It can literally create a fully built-out treasure trove of link awesomeness on every one of your WordPress pages. (Great for product category pages; best for folks who want control over the "style" of their blog.)

Action Step: Choose an Etsy store WordPress plugin to create a virtual replica of your store on your blog.

Blog Hack No.2: Become an Email Autoresponder Ninja

An email what? But wait…I thought we were building a blog here. Nobody said anything about EMAIL!

Here's the thing though: By far the most reliable, consistent and cost-effective way to continually market to your leads & customers is through email. (Sorry, Facebook and Twitter…but email is still where it's at.)

And one of the best (and cheapest) ways to

collect those ever-valuable email addresses is through visitors to your blog.

I doubled my sales in a month by simply putting an email opt-in form, with text that said, "Sign Up For Exclusive Discounts," in places such as:

- The body of my blog posts
- A custom widget in my sidebar
- The footer of every blog post
- Every product category page
- The header of my blog

The only problem was that I wish I had done it sooner!

What you DON'T want to do is handle the collection and sending of all these emails yourself.

Your email account will get blacklisted, and, frankly who wants to deal with all that stress?

Instead you want to sign up for an email autoresponder service, which will let you create automated messages that go out to every new subscriber when they opt in to your list.

I've got months of pre-generated email messages letting all my new subscribers know about all the cool stuff they can buy from me.

There are many companies that can handle this for you. Some even charge you up to $300/month — with a $2000 sign-up fee. Ouch!

My personal autoresponder of choice is Aweber. They're cheap, I only pay $19.99 a month — and they're really **easy** to use. (And they've got a $1.00 trial to see if you like them.)

Whatever you do, make sure you choose somebody to handle this important part of your overall blog marketing strategy.

Action Step: Choose an email autoresponder service, if you don't already have one, such as Aweber or MailChimp to handle your email marketing needs.

Blog Hack No.3: Make Your Blog Super Share-able

Crafty Social Buttons is a super simple, but surprisingly powerful, plugin that lets people easily share your products, blog posts, pictures — anything on your blog! — by placing a row of colorful social network icons in the body of your blog content and in the footer of your blog.

Unlike most other tools, these icons look very handcraft-y and artisanal. Not the usual boring web 2.0 stuff that's out there.

And the cool thing is, once you set it up, you don't have to even think about it anymore.

Action Step: *Add the Crafty Social Buttons plug-in to your WordPress blog.*

Blog Hack No.4: Embrace the Pinterest Tribe

So, we all know how powerful Pinterest can be when promoting our Etsy store. (Or at least I hope we know.)

Shameless plug: If not, feel free to get a refresher course by picking up my "How to Sell on Etsy With Pinterest" book at CraftBizInsider.com/Pinterest)

And one of the quickest and easiest ways to build your loyal Pinterest army is to have "pin it" icons hover over each image on your blog.

There are quite a few plugins that handle this duty, but one of my faves is the Pinterest Pin It Button for Images Plugin. Not only is it easy to use, but it's FREE of charge with no hidden upsell. (Many FREE plugins hide many of their best features behind a sneaky paywall.)

Action Step: *Add a Pin It icon plugin to your blog, let your customers do some free promotion for you.*

Blog Hack No.5: Get Some Facebook Likes

Everybody is on Facebook. (And I do mean everybody.)

The simplest way to crack through the guarded halls of the Facebook universe is to have blog visitors follow your page and share and like your content.

Unfortunately, you've got to make it dead easy for people to do this. That's why you need some kind of plugin that puts Facebook like buttons and "Follow Me" on Facebook buttons on your blog.

There are a ton of plugins that offer this

functionality, with varying levels of success.

One of the simplest, but most reliable, offerings is the simply-named Facebook Like Button plugin.

The cool thing about this plugin is it not only allows you to place all that Facebook awesomeness on your blog…

But it also lets you choose the button position — not all Facebook icons are created equal — and gives you control over the look and feel of the icon image.

I've found varying results depending on the icon type I choose.

Action Step: Add a Facebook like button to your blog, with the Facebook like button plug-in. I have the most success with Facebook icons in the right sidebar, but you may find better results with another position.

Blog Hack No.6: Get Somebody Else to Install This Stuff for You

Yes, you could learn all about the dizzying array

of WordPress plugins and autoresponder opt-in JavaScript code options out there. And I have…mostly because I know just enough to break my blog a few times a year.

But again, I don't want you to get hung up in the technology. It's not that important you master it, especially when all the bells and whistles will change in three years anyway.

So reach out to that web developer you found on Upwork and ask them to install and customize these plugins for you.

This job should be even easier than the last one; all they have to do is upload a couple of zip files and tweak a few settings.

And then, later, if you have some extra free time and are bored of counting all your new profits, feel free to become a Ph.D. in WordPress studies.

Until then…let somebody else handle the non-creative stuff.

Action Step: *Let somebody handle all the website plug-in stuff for you.*

Chapter 2 Key Takeaways:

- **Nothing will make you more money than replicating your Etsy store onto your blog.** Etsy Shop WordPress Plugin and Etsy Treasure Posting Tool Plugin are two great plug-ins to help with that.

- **Signing up for an email autoresponder**, such as Aweber, will help you turn blog visitors into new leads — with virtually no effort on your part.

- **Crafty Social Buttons is a fantastic plug-in** to help your customers share your amazing products with their friends and family.

- **The Pinterest Pin It Button for Images Plugin is another fantastic social sharing tool** that allows your customers to easily pin every image on your blog.

- **The Facebook Like Button plugin might be the most important social sharing plug-in of all.** Not only does it boost visibility of your store, but it also keeps your customers on your blog longer. (More opportunities to sell stuff.)

- **The Facebook Like Button plugin might be the most important social sharing plug-in of all.** Not only does it boost visibility of your store, but it also keeps your customers on your blog longer. (More opportunities to sell stuff.)

Chapter 3: Setting Up Your Etsy Blog Storefront

"Many a small thing has been made large by the right kind of advertising."

-Mark Twain

Those blog hacks should get you off to a great start —but this is where things are about to get **really** interesting.

You see, blogs are basically your own little patches of online real estate. Think of it like your garden that grows fresh herbs: the more you work the land, pull the weeds, use awesome-smelling fertilizer (I just love a whiff of THAT in the morning!), and dedicate time and energy …the more you're going to reap the rewards.

I've said it before –I'll say it again: blogs are CRAZY easy to run, once you've gotten the wheels off the tarmac.

So, essentially, we just need to get that new blog of yours into a great-looking skin, and seamlessly integrated into your Etsy storefront.

Now there are quite a few ways you can make this happen – but fear not, my fellow Etsian: You ARE NOT alone in feeling like this isn't your gig.

Take a quick gander on any Etsy forums, discussing blogging… you'll quickly find just how many of your fellow Etsians are just not interested in learning coding and HTML.

My people… you are not alone. Yet still, take heart: This isn't going to be as difficult as you might think. Quite frankly this is going to be WAY easier than it looks. Trust me, I'm not fond of technical babble…

So without further ado, and anymore discussion of HTML, here's my three-step process to setting up your Etsy store on your blog.

Step No.1: Get Your House in Order

My father used to say: "Never ask a hard worker how to do things. Always ask the lazy guy. They'll get it done in half the time with half the work."

So, how would we set-up an herb garden so that it succeeds —while minimizing the work and time involved?

Simple: Run an irrigation system, so all you need to do is turn a valve, *rather than actively standing there with a hose.*

Now, let's think of your Etsy shop as the soil itself. It's where you plant the seeds (your products) and harvest (via PayPal).

Your blog, on the other hand, is your sunlight, your fertilizer, your irrigation system, and unfortunately… there are the weeds (spam).

Do Etsy Gardening the RIGHT Way…Till the Soil First.

True efficiency and success usually comes down

to how you set things up in the first place. All too often, I see e-commerce sites that are just too dang confusing, too complex and the customer has to jump through WAY too many hoops to purchase a product (i.e.: GoDaddy anyone?)

This is one reason why I am a big believer in blog designs that are beautiful, creative, eye-catching …yet simple.

They're also easy to navigate, and if someone is interested in purchasing something from your Etsy shop… then by all means, make it SO unbelievably easy to get them to that giant "buy" button of yours.

The Power of Etsy Organization

One of Etsy's big selling points is how they provide us sellers with store sections. These sections not only allow you to direct people to exactly what they're looking for, but you can harness your specific sections into keywords –to get big, bad Google's attention.

So, here's what I want you to do (and these instructions can also be found in Etsy's help section):

1. **Determine what your inventory looks like** – try to come up with 3-5 different categories that describe your product offerings accurately. Don't get too specific, just use common sense.

2. **In Etsy, go to *"Your Shop"* and then *"Sections."***
3. **Focus on editing your sections,** categorizing your inventory, and naming your products in an enticing, but logical way.

Being able to categorize your shop offers two major advantages:

- **You can channel customers,** who are looking for something in specific – to a place where you know they'll find what they want.
- **You can feature these sections** on specific pages in your blog. The catch: You're going to need to purchase Etsy Pro, which will run you about $40 tops.

Quick Tip ESSENTIAL

I will bullhorn this to the Etsian masses: HAVE

A FEATURED ITEM SECTION!

You'll notice the *"Sections"* page didn't have a way for you to do this – but you can actually create a *"Featured Items"* section in your Etsy shop by simply following these steps:

1. Click on the *"Your Shop"* link.
2. Go to the listings you want to feature.
3. In the table that displays listings, you'll see a star to the right of the date that the listing is set to expire.
4. Click on the star, and that item will be displayed on your main storefront at the top.

When a customer sees these featured items, it will show up under "FEATURED ITEMS FROM (YOUR_AWESOME_SHOP_NAME)."

Now, we've setup the groundwork…this Etsy-blog integration just got WAY easier…

Step No.2: Add a Touch of Etsian Class

I talked a bit before about how to apply a skin (or a paint job) to your blog. If anything, you should probably do this BEFORE you start getting into the nitty-gritty of Etsy-blog integration. That way, you've already captured the look you're going for.

This is kind of a rehashing of what I talked about before —when I gave you several places you could go to purchase themes. But here's a little tidbit I decided to save until now…

Here It Comes…Wait For IT!

Did you know you can actually purchase WordPress themes ON ETSY??

I kid you not! What better place than to purchase your Etsy theme from a fellow Etsy seller, who knows Etsy —because they're running their own Etsy business, SELLING ETSY THEMES!

Yet still, before you go bonkers and purchase a nice eye-popping, shiny new Etsy theme —be sure you follow these basic rules.

1. **Make sure your Etsy theme looks professionally done**. DO NOT skimp on this, people. Failure here will hurt you down the road.
2. **Make sure your Etsy theme follows the artistic flow and feel of your target market**, your specific niche, and your inventory. It's about

consistency and not confusing your customers. Which brings me to number three…

3.   Make sure your Etsy theme is simple and easy to understand. DO NOT make this thing too complex or too busy –it's such a shame when a visitor could have been willing to buy but doesn't, because getting to your POS (Point of Sale) was too difficult.

Step No.3: Make It Easy for Them to "Show You The Money"

Okay, now for the moment we've all been waiting for…

Setting up your blog is going to be super easy, since we just setup your Etsy shop ahead of time.

The reason why this is the case is because any WordPress plugin you use works basically the same way:

They don't *create a whole new shop*. They simply copy the one you've already got, and then reproduce it beautifully on your own blog page.

Thus, if you've setup your Etsy shop correctly, then you've just made your bloggin' life easy.)

Now, there are a few plug-ins you can use to this end. Unfortunately, the free ones and official WP plug-ins, such as Etsy Mini aren't going to be as comprehensive as you might need them to be (unless you're just trying to advertise your Etsy business on your blog —and not *feature* the shop itself ON your blog like an e-commerce site).

This is why Etsians are turning to a FANTASTIC WordPress plugin, called Etsy Pro. I've mentioned it before, but now I'm going to show you how to harness this fantastic tool.

Back to my garden analogy: Plug-ins like Etsy Mini are like using a watering hose; plug-ins like Etsy Pro are like installing a full-blown irrigation system.

Let's just say, they call it "Pro" for a reason…because this baby's gonna take you into the big leagues!

Now, it is possible for you to simply get your VA (Virtual Assistant) on the task so you can save some time —because this can get a bit technical. However, as always, I'll just be real with you… it's really a piece of cake.

Also, not only are there tons of tutorials and

videos out there to show you the ropes, but many an Etsian blogger has touched on the how-to's of using Etsy Pro. I'm just going to say – the initial setup should only take you a couple minutes, even if you have NO CLUE what you're doing.

Here are just a couple of basic steps:

1. **Download the .zip file of the plugin**. (For Mac users –Don't allow the file to automatically unzip… that's WordPress's job, so be sure to kill that option.)

2. **Load the plugin into WP under the "*Plug-ins*" section**, selecting *Add New*.

3. **Once it's done loading, now you need to type your Etsy shop name** into where you setup the plugin.

4. **This is where it gets a little complicated,** but everywhere that sells Etsy Pro *should have a setup tutorial*. If they don't, then just go to someone else who does. (I literally watched a girl on YouTube set up Etsy Pro in less than five minutes flat. Seriously, it's super easy, and the technical part is all cut and paste stuff.)

Sections in Shortcode (Don't Panic, It's Super Easy)

Once this is up and running —now all you need to do is setup your Etsy shop sections on Etsy Pro. (Now you'll see why I told you to do this at the beginning of the chapter).

This part can seem a bit difficult —but again, a quick search for tutorials on this and you'll have 15 different ones pop up on YouTube.

Basically, where you see the "short code" for the Etsy Pro plugin for that particular page —all you need to do is replace *"Section Name,"* with the desired name of your section on your shop page (i.e.: Fancy Cardigans).

Again, this is all cut and paste kind of work, and while it may seem a little daunting in the beginning, you'll be a WP plugin pro within 30 minutes of light research on YouTube University.

Here's How This Should Look...

Once that's done, now you can step back and take a look at what you've got.

You will notice if you set up your blog and your Etsy shop correctly, you'll have a separate page for every Etsy section you have.

Remember the "Featured" section? Well, because of your due diligence, that featured section should show up on your blog –just as displayed on your main Etsy shop page.

The listings themselves will appear kind of like those your Etsy shop, just now, it's in your awesome blog theme –and when you click on an item, that listing is still within your blog and you remain inside the blog page itself (without an annoying redirect to a different website).

Now keep in mind, it is only when a customer clicks on the big green button to buy the product that your blog directs them over to your actual Etsy shop.

This happens because it's against Etsy rules to feature your shop on your blog, while directing them to some other checkout counter –it's kinda like depriving Etsy out of a sale, so I can understand their point of view. Besides, that customer already hit the green button, so it's not much more of a jump for them to finalize the purchase in Etsy.

Well, congratulations –your patch of online

garden is tilled, your irrigation system is all setup and your herbs are facing south.

You just made life easy for you and your customers —not to mention streamlining how quickly your profits flow into your PayPal account.

Chapter 3 Key Takeaways:

- **The first, and most important, step to prepping your blog for sales is to get your Etsy store organized.** Spend time ensuring your inventory, and most notably your sections, are named accurately and with a touch of creativity.

- **If you're not overly jazzed about the current look of your blog, then check out Etsy to find WordPress themes to decorate your online property.** Be sure that the theme you choose looks professional, has simple functionality, and fits the vibe of your product offering.

- **The best plug-in for installing your Etsy store on your blog is the Etsy Pro plug-in.** Though it does cost nearly $40, it's a great addition to your Etsy seller toolbox.

Chapter 4:
Okay, But What Do I Blog About?

"If things seem under control, you're just not going fast enough."

-Mario Andretti

Okay, the boring grunt work is done. You have officially gotten past the number one hurdle most people complain about when setting up their blog which is...

The technical crap!

Did you survive? Are you still breathing? Is your creative soul stay intact as we set up your autoresponders and plug-ins and short codes?

Good. I knew you could do it.

Because, now we get to the fun part. Which is creating fabulous, amazing, wonderful — and ultimately profitable — content for your blog.

"Content, It's What's for Dinner"

Content is one of those buzzwords Internet "experts" like to throw around. Like "engagement" and "authenticity" and "platform."

But website content is really just the text, images, video and other forms of rich media that users consume while visiting your website.

And it's really, really important.

Because content is the STUFF that gets shared. Content is the STUFF that provides the emotional connection to your future customers.

Content is what helps your web visitors forget that you're actually **selling** to them.

There was a time in the not-so-distant past when

blog content meant little more than horrible 500-word articles about random keyword-optimized topics — browse the archives of Ezine Articles for an example of this low-grade content sludge.

But these days content can mean:

- Videos showcasing your work station or a behind-the-scenes look at your shop.
- Audio files of customer testimonials raving about your products.
- High-quality pictures of your latest creation.
- A blog post on how you got started — and tips to help other creative types get started with their business.
- YouTube videos, not created by you, that you embed in your blog.
- Polls, contests and sweepstakes — anything that gets people off their butt and getting interactive.
- Anything to do with children or pets. (I swear these are like blog catnip.)

Even sales pages and product galleries CAN be content...if it's presented in a fun and interesting way. (The website Woot of the Day has a "daily deal" whose description alone is worth the read.)

So, now you've gotten a bit of a peek at what's possible, here are my FIVE tips to creating consistent blog content that attracts leads, moves visitors and helps you sell more stuff…

Blog Content Tip No.1: Utilize Your Strengths

This one should be fairly obvious, but I'm shocked by how many Etsy sellers resist blogging, because they don't like to write blog posts.

Okay, then….so don't write blog posts.

If you like to do webcam videos, then embrace your inner teenager and express yourself on camera. If you like to take pictures, then pull out your DSLR and start shooting those pics.

If you like to write haikus about magical kitty cats, then don't let me stand in your way. (Who knows…you might even create a whole sub-niche of followers.)

The key is to ask yourself honestly: What's the best way for you, or members of your team, to express yourself?

For me, I really like VIDEO and WRITING. (So the ideal mix for me is to do behind-the-scenes videos and short, opinionated blog posts.)

I'm not that into pictures. I'm a really bad photographer and the whole camera thing bores me. So I have my assistant/college intern handle the picture-taking side of things.

Whatever you do, try to get in a mix of highly-visual stuff (video and images) with SOME meatier text-driven stuff (blog rants and links to other cool stuff). This will give your visitors numerous different ways to discover you.

Action Step: Make a list of the 2-3 forms of content creation that you or your team feels most comfortable with. Make sure some form of pretty visuals are in there somewhere.)

Blog Content Tip No.2: Brainstorm Them Content Categories

There's a reason I love blogs so much. (As opposed to your run-of-the-mill website.)

Because BLOGS have this wonderful organizational structure — based around categories — that make grouping your content into themes really easy.

Good for you, good for your visitors and good for the search engines.

Which is why Google loves blogs so much.

The trick is to come up with these blog categories early enough in the creation of your blog, so you have a road map for the content you want to create.

And not simply just writing whatever you want.

The categories that YOU choose will depend on your business. But here are a couple I think every Etsy seller SHOULD have in their blog back pocket:

- **A category for each section of your Etsy store offering**. If you only sell one product, then obviously a general "Shopping" category would be fine. But if you sell many different kinds of products — or have one product, with many different themes —

think about breaking them up into separate categories.

- **A "Promotions" category**. These are great for housing all your special sales, contest offers and whatever other cool little marketing idea you come up with to promote on your blog.

- **A "Behind the Scenes" category.** People just love this stuff. (God knows why, I'd be bored to tears of a video about my garage.) But think about creating a category that gives your fans a sneak peek at how the Etsy sausage is made.

- **A "Personal" category** for rants, opinions and content that isn't focused exactly on your Etsy store. Again, I resisted this for a while thinking nobody cares. Not true! They do care, especially if you express something you're passionate about. (Like the need for more art education in school.) Some of the biggest explosions in leads I've gotten have been from these types of blog posts…which had nothing to do with my products.

- **A "Gallery" category**. Like I said, I'm no shutterbug. But people love galleries and photos. So if you decide to do a lot of them, think about collecting all your photos into one centralized place.

- **A "Design" or "Ideas" category**. This one's really fun and can get quite a bit of interest from your blog community. I like to put sketches, designs, and photos of products I'm THINKING about creating. (There are a ton of apps that can do this all from your smartphone.) Then, I usually have people vote on them by leaving comments in the Facebook comments section. (Which also gets my website in front of a lot more eyeballs.)

- **A "Tips" or "Advice" category**. The one thing you'll find out pretty quickly with your blog is that people don't just see you as somebody who creates some products in their craft room. You are the living embodiment of the American Dream: Making money off your creativity. (Even if it sometimes feels like that "money" is hard to find.) So anything you can do to give back to your community in the way of advice or inspiration always pays you back ten-fold.

Note: It's always better to have fewer categories than too many categories. (I learned this lesson the hard way.) You want to have simple, easily understood categories that help organize your content — not make it as cluttered as a teenage boy's bedroom.

Blog Content Tip No.3: Come Up With a Zillion Content Ideas in 20 Minutes or Less

Okay, maybe not a zillion. But quite a few. (And it's way simpler than you think.)

There have been a TON of blog posts — and I do mean a ton — written on the subject of coming up with topics for your blog.

A couple of my favorites are these two: "50 Can't-Fail Techniques for Finding Blog Topics" by Copy Blogger and "5 Ways to Brainstorm New Blog Topics" from BluAdz.

But here are a couple that I use ALL the time:

- **Do a product review or book review**. Is there something you're reading or watching? Feel free to give your honest feedback on it. (People just love book reviews. Especially on video.)

- **Create a regular feature**. This could be as simple as "You Know You're an Etsy Seller When…" to "Things My Jack Russell Terrier Does."

- **Write a how-to guide or series of tips about anything**. I don't care what it is…could be finding a good plumber or getting your LLC, somebody out there has had to do it too. Write a simple blog post about what you learned along the way, and how you can save other people the trouble.

(Trust me: Stuff like this gets shares A LOT and boosts the goodwill toward your brand.)

- **Create some Google Alerts around topics related to your Etsy products**. If you're not familiar with Google Alerts, it's a great way to create filtered alerts around specific keywords that are then emailed to your inbox. So, whatever you sell — from dollhouses to soap to velvet Elvis caricatures — create an alert and become the de facto "expert" in your product field.

- **Talk about your obstacles and challenges**. People love to hear about people overcoming problems. (And, as business owners, we got plenty of those.)

- **Ask "What's missing" from a particular topic or debate**? This is a great way to look at things from a different perspective…and get lots of interest too. I wrote a post called "Why Wal-Mart is good for Etsy sellers," that got quite a passionate response.

- **Talk about national trends**. Can you tie in something about the economy, politics or culture to your store? You don't have to go on a political rant, just echo what people are already talking about.

Blog Content Tip No.4: Come Up With a Blog Post Calendar

There's an expression that goes: "What gets scheduled, gets done." And it's totally true.

I fought this concept for a while. As a creative type, I didn't want to force myself into another to-do list, especially around my blog. I wanted the freedom to be able to produce whatever content I wanted.

Guess what happened…yep, I didn't produce anything at all.

The key is to have a consistent production of blog content, which you then promote on social media (more on that later), which creates more entryways for your future customers to be led into your business.

Now, inevitably when creating a calendar for your blog there is ONE question that comes up: How OFTEN should you blog?

Which is really just a fancy way of asking:

"What's the LEAST I can do and still get results?"

In my opinion, I think the sweet spot is to blog 1-2 times a week. (Any less than that and it just won't work.) But remember, these don't have to 1200-word essays. They can be almost anything, you just have to schedule it and be consistent.

Here's a look at my sample calendar:

Week 1: Monday - Product Spotlight [Image]; Thursday - How-To Tip [Text]
Week 2: Monday - Google Alerts/Trends [Text]; Thursday - Behind-the-Scenes [Video]
Week 3: Monday - Customer Spotlight; Thursday - Product Review [Video]
Week 4: Monday - Product Ideas/Designs or Promotion; Thursday - Obstacles Overcome [Text]

Now you'll notice I don't do a lot of outright selling and pitching. That is by design.

I do have posts that specifically promote something like the Product Spotlight in Week 1 or the Promotion in Week 4. But otherwise it's just straight content.

And even my customer spotlight, with behind-the-scenes videos, isn't selling. (Even though it's helping build my brand.)

The biggest thing I'm doing is creating content that can be shared all around the social media universe.

Which is where the REAL bang for your blogging buck comes from.

Now, you don't have to be this aggressive when starting out. Maybe you want to just start out by posting once a week.

But the cool thing about having a schedule like this is it sort of prepares my brain for what's coming…so when I do sit down to create the content, I'm pretty much ready to go.

And don't forget to put the type of media your blog post will be. This will ensure you are hitting all of your blogging bases and reaching your audience in a number of different mediums.

Blog Content Tip No.5: Just Do It!

This last tip is really simple. Follow through on your calendar.

If you find yourself falling behind, then feel free to outsource it. (You could hire somebody off a site like Upwork, or maybe find a poor college student in your hometown who'd like to make a few extra few bucks.)

The great thing is: You've already got your calendar created. Now you can simply hand over this calendar to your team.

Just make sure that whoever is creating the content for your blog represents you and your brand well. Because this stuff can spread really quickly, which is what we're going to cover in the next chapter.

Chapter 4 Action Steps:

- **Figure out what you like to do — whether it's video, text or pictures — and do lots of that on your blog.** Don't pigeonhole yourself into a type of media you simply don't enjoy.

- **Brainstorm 5 to 7 categories that you'd like to cover in the content of your blog.** This could be as simple as "behind-the-scenes," "creative inspiration," or "new promotions" — or as off-the-wall as "pictures of my dog" or "crazy weird things people put on Etsy."

- **Come up with 150 million block topic ideas.** You could do almost anything — a manifesto, a crafty tutorial, a video book review, a behind-the-scenes look at your craft room, etc. Anything that shares your point of view is good.

- **Create a blogging editorial calendar...that you'll actually stick to.** By scheduling specific topics for certain days of the month, you'll increase the likelihood that you actually follow through with creating that awesome blog content.

- **Follow through!** By creating blog content on a consistent basis, you'll not only strengthen your habit of creation, but you will also create expectancy in your customers. (Which can lead to increased sales!)

Chapter 5:
The Ultimate Blog Content Checklist

"Nothing is so contagious as enthusiasm."

- Samuel Taylor Coleridge

It's all well and great to create fantastic blog content. But it's another getting actual human beings to read it, view it, or share it with their (somewhat) closest friends.

And while we shouldn't obsess and spend hours worrying about how to promote our blog posts — we've got other important things to do, like make more Etsy products — it is important to realize that there are a few simple, but important, things we can do when publishing our content to make its discover-ability much, much easier.

So that's what we're going to cover in this chapter.

Here is my ultimate, FIVE step blog publishing checklist to ensure you get all the blog content thing for your promotion buck:

Checklist Item No.1: Sprinkle Your Content with Keywords

Now, keywords are not quite as important to blog content as they used to be way back in the Mesozoic era — or as I like to call it, 2007.

But keywords and phrases are *still* relevant – you just don't want to overuse them. (And by overusing, I mean stuffing your 300-word blog post with 25 keywords.)

If anything, you're going to want to use what are called, "long tail keywords." I agree, they sound like something you might hear about on Sesame Street – but in fact, they are useful for SEO purposes.

- Here's a normal keyword example: "handmade bags"

- Here's a long tail keyword example: "custom handmade leather bags on Etsy"

Essentially, the strength of long tail keywords is two-fold. First, it's better for SEO purposes, because it places your target market under laser focus and lessens your competition for a single keyword.

Second, it attracts visitors who are searching SPECIFICALLY for that keyword, increasing the likelihood that the individual could become a customer.

Good places for these keywords?

Here's where I would like you to place your keywords, at the minimum:

- The title of your blog post (the most important placement for your keywords).
- The first paragraph of your blog post (if you can get it in the first sentence, even better).
- The last paragraph of your blog post.

And that's about it. No need to stress it.

And again, the focus should be on good content. But if you're going to go to the trouble of creating this content, why not optimize it so people — and future customers — can find it?

Checklist Item No.2: A WordPress Image Tells 1000 Words

Chances are, you're going to have a ton of photos in your blog posts. Whether it's to feature your latest products, or just a cute picture of your Jack Russell Terrier waging war on a pillow case, visual media — such as photos — are a fantastic way to boost engagement, increase readership and generate more sales.

But there's one secret/hidden benefit that images have — which many Etsy sellers fail to capitalize on. They can boost the SEO impact of your page big-time and help get some serious traffic to your blog, by optimizing the following:

- Filename
- Alt tag

- Caption

Let's dig into these little bit deeper.

What's in a (File) Name?

So one thing that many Etsy sellers don't know, is that WHAT you name the photos that you upload has a direct bearing on how well your blog post performs in the search rankings.

This means before inserting your photo into a blog post, you'll want to change the name of the photo from some generic default title — such as "photo_one.JPEG" — to something more keyword-rich such as "decorative_Christmas_candle.JPEG."

Now, it goes without saying that you want to be ethical and accurate. If your photo has nothing to do with what you're titling it, not only will you not get much benefit from the search engines — you might actually get penalized.

Google does this all the time.

But as long as you play straight, you'll get

quite a bit benefit from this tactic.

And how you change the file name your photo?

Simple. Just double-click on the photo inside the field where the name is designated. Wait for the named to be highlighted type in your new name — use hyphens and underscores instead of spaces — and you'll be good to go.

What the Heck Is an Alt Tag and Why Should I Care?

The alt tag is simply a text description of what an image or video is about. It's used to help visually-impaired web users determine the content of particular page. (Unlike a 300-word blog post, Google can't easily figure out what an image is by simply scanning it for keywords.)

Adding alt tag to your images is dead easy. (Even though most marketers totally forget to fill them in.)

When inserting a new photo into a blog post, look below the "title" field and you'll see the "alternate text" field. Typing your keyword-rich alt tag there.

For updating the all tags of existing images, simply edit the post in the back end of your blog: click on the image, click on the edit image button and then an "advanced" tab will open up, then simply type in your alt tag text.

Caption This

Captions aren't quite as important as the first two elements of an image's properties. But they can still provide a nice additional search engine boost. As marketers with meager marketing budgets, we can take all the free advertising we can get!

When inserting an image into a WordPress post, you have the option filling in a caption. All you want to do is to come up with a brief sentence that describes the image and includes some keyword.

Don't go overboard, making it robotic. Just write a natural description of the image — or the blog post itself — and include one or more keywords that can help the visibility of your blog post.

Checklist Item No. 3: Going Meta

A meta description is actually rather easy to find, and no, you don't have to be logged in to WordPress in order to see one. Here's how to see an example:

- Go to Google and type a phrase into the search bar.

- Find a listing that catches your eye. (Let's assume that you found a WordPress site.)

- Now look under the title (big blue) and under the URL (small green).

- That black-colored text right there... is likely a meta description that was purposely typed into the box.

Now, though the meta-description does not directly affect the search engine optimization of your blog post — Google has removed it entirely from its algorithm due to spam abuse — it still makes a huge impact.

Because it's what humans see.

Just as you scanned the listings, so will your prospective customers. So take a bit of time to craft a meta-description that's engaging, interesting and promises the benefit of the blog post.

And where do you fill in the meta-description?

In the back end of each WordPress blog post, below the main text box, you will see a meta-description field. Just fill in there.

By default, WordPress will pull the first 60 to 75 characters of your blog post as the meta-description. (Which may or may not be advantageous to your blog post promotion.)

Either way, I find the two minutes it takes me to write up a quick meta-description is usually worth it in terms of added block traffic in additional sales.

Checklist Item No.4: The Power of the Title

Let's just say – if there's any item in this checklist that's fighting for first place importance: IT'S YOUR TITLE.

It's that bright, shining beacon at the top of the page.

It's what shows up as the attention grabber from Facebook to Twitter

It's how you hook in the unsuspecting reader – making them think, "Hmm… what are the 3 Best Ways To Make a Spoon Ring?"

It's the best thing since sliced bread and the bee's knees.

It's your title!

Not only does your title have the opportunity to grab the attention of Google… again, I'd heartily recommend using a long tail keyword for this puppy (BUT DON'T SOUND SPAMMISH).

Why shall ye not sound of the spammish? Because, much like for your meta description, this is going to be seen by people – and ultimately, that's the real traffic you're looking for in the first place.

Based on my own experience, here are just a few quick tips on how to have an attention-grabbing title:

- Keep your title short, sweet and to the point.
- Make it sexy: use alliterations, puns and avoid repeating redundant words that you mention more than once (see what I did there?)
- Hit it with a little SEO.
- Keep it accurate, because facts sell.
- Use numbers.

Honestly, using numbers in titles (7 Awesome Date Ideas) is almost so effective it's scary. If my example in the last sentence were a link –I'd probably try to click on it.

In Conclusion

If you follow this checklist –your efforts are going to go a long way. Essentially, if you do your due diligence, you can market like an SEO master, write like a pro blogger, and inspire like an Etsian.

Not bad in a day's work, to say the least. Of course, you're probably saying yourself: but what about back links? What about social media?

Well, therein lies a beautiful transition…

Chapter 5 Action Steps:

- **Don't forget about them keywords.** Key places to include keywords include the title of your blog post, the first paragraph and the last paragraph.

- **Images are one of the most important ways to boost traffic to your blog posts.** Be sure to pay particular attention to the filename, alt tag and caption for each image you included a blog post. (Don't forget those keywords!)

- **Meta-descriptions may not boost the Google ranking of your blog posts, but they're important because they attract eyeballs.** Take a few extra minutes to craft an interesting meta-description to pull interested, curious web surfers to your blog content.

- **The title is the most important promotional element of your blog post.**

The keywords are important, be sure to write a catchy, interesting title that will hook readers in just a matter of seconds. (Focusing on benefits is always a good way to go.)

Chapter 6:
Promoting Your Blog Posts (in 5 Minutes or Less)

"If your actions inspire others to dream more, learn more, do more and become more, you are a leader."

- John Quincy Adams

In the last chapter –I showed you how to please the big, bad Google. In this chapter, we're going to talk about a way to please...well, real *people*.

If you were just blogging to capture the attention of a search-engine crawler bot, then you're probably reading the **wrong** book.

But, that's why I am an absolute fan of social

media (well, at least for it's ability to be a fan-freaking-tastic marketing tool).

No platform offers as many real people, and genuine eyeballs, like social media.

And the cool part is, every single piece of content that we create on our blog can be shared and promoted on various social media properties — with just the click of a button.

Now you *may* see varying results with different social media platforms. Personally, I find I get a lot of consistent traction with Facebook; Twitter seems to be more sporadic.

But, if you follow a simple formula — like the one I'm about to give you — and use it each time you create a new piece of blog content, you'll find your blog, your store and your message will be reaching thousands of people in no time.

So here is my FIVE step blog promotion blueprint:

Blueprint Method No.1: Long Live the Facebook

Facebook marketing is a huge topic; I actually wrote an **entire book** about how to market your Etsy store on Facebook. (Shameless plug: You can pick up a copy over at CraftBizInsider.com/fbook)

But here is Facebook marketing, for us Etsy sellers, in a nutshell:

1.   Share lots of our cool blog content on our Facebook page…
2.   So we get lots of new Facebook fans…
3.   Which we can then turn into email subscribers, leads and new customers.

That's really as complicated as it gets. Sure there are lots of cool nifty Facebook tactics, tricks and tools and plug-ins and apps, but really it comes down to attracting fans and turning those fans into people who pay us money for our creations.

So here's what I recommend you do:

- **Create a great piece of blog content**
(make sure it has a schnazzy and attractive

title).

- **Create a really attractive photo** — or have someone created for you — that you can use when promoting your blog post on Facebook. The ideal size of the photo is 400 pixels by 400 pixels. (If you can add a small line of text that echoes the title of the blog post, even better.)

- **Post a status update to your Facebook fan page**, with a link to the blog post and upload an optimized 400 pixel by 400 pixel photo.

Now if you have thousands of engaged, passionate fan page fans, then there's a good chance you won't have to "advertise" your blog post to the Facebook universe.

Unfortunately, most of the time you may have to pay five or $10 to "boost" the visibility of your post. (Don't worry, if you do just a couple of these a week, before you know it you'll start to get a ton of readership to your blog.)

The best thing is:

If you're able to set up Facebook like buttons on your blog, as well as an email opt-in box, then you're likely to capture leads from Facebook fans and non-fans alike.

And when you get a little bit of engagement baked into your Facebook fan page, advertising your products, special offers and juicy coupons becomes a lot easier — and a lot cheaper.

Some of the biggest profits I've made have been from limited time Facebook coupon offers. (Again, check out my "How to Sell on Etsy With Facebook" guide for more detailed information on how to use Facebook effectively sell more Etsy goods.)

Blueprint Method No.2: Not Bad Fer a Tweet 'er Two

Let's be honest, as these social media networks begin to mount up – it seems like this is going to take a TON of work. But, I say again, have no fear.

There's an app for that…well, if not, at least there's a company with a dashboard of handy doohickeys.

For instance, HootSuite has been one of my favorite (free) social media marketing platforms out there — for the simple fact that it links all these networks into one single place.

From your dashboard you can simultaneously blast updates, posts, pictures, videos, etc. and HootSuite will even pick the best time of day for them to go out.

Also, Facebook and Twitter are now so unbelievably intertwined that you're looking at a HUGE base of possible exposure.

However — much like blog titles — you've got to keep things interesting and short. People have no attention span anymore.

Here's what I do when promoting blog content on Twitter:

- **Always start with a brief description of what kind of content medium** the blog post is. Example: [BLOG] or [VIDEO] or [PIC].

- **Then jump right into what readers can expect to get from your blog post.** Example: "Five tips when creating a Star Wars sock monkey." "Shocking photo evidence that my cat hates Justin Bieber."

- **Then place a link to the blog post.** You can use a URL shortener, if you run out of room.

- **And then follow it up with a #hashtag.** I like to do #Etsy, but you could use any # that you think people might use to find your content.

And even if nobody retweets your blog content and even if thousands of people don't rush off to see your blog post immediately, tweeting out a link to your blog post will definitely help its search-engine ranking.

I see amazing things happen in Google after I tweet out a link to my blog post.

Blueprint Method No.3: Get Socially Bookmarked

So a lot of marketers will use the first two blueprint methods I've outlined, but that's where they stop. Which is unfortunate, because there are quite a few other nifty little promotional methods we can use to get our message out there.

One of the more interesting methods, within social media spheres, has to undoubtedly be sites like StumbleUpon (a favorite among Etsians).

These sites aren't quite social media platforms in the traditional sense. But they allow people to quickly search — or stumble — blogs, websites, or almost anything on the web that may pique their interest.

When they do find something they like, they bookmark it.

And you are given a small, but powerful, endorsement of your blog.

At the same time, sites like these are also social-voting networks – sort of the same way you get "likes" on Facebook.

In the case of StumbleUpon, you have an opportunity for something to go EXTREMELY viral **very** quickly if you get a bunch of votes in your favor.

Getting your blog posts some real traction on sites like StumbleUpon isn't something that happens overnight. You've got to work at it.

But it's effort that usually pays off…big! (A feature spot on StumbleUpon can lead to thousands and thousands of new visitors right away.

So here's what I would do:

- **Sign up for a StumbleUpon account.** Start stumbling & bookmarking sites, Etsy stores, and blogs that have a similar look and feel as your blog.

- **Each time you create a new piece of content** on your blog, bookmark it on these two social voting platforms.

- **Bonus points:** Engage with the

communities on sites like these and see if you can't "lobby" your way into the top rankings of their recommended sites.

Also, just like with the Twitter promotion strategy, even if you don't get immediate results in terms of visitors, you **will** see a HUGE bump in your search engine rankings for your blog posts.

Blueprint method No.4: Pinterest – Because It's Pinterest

If there were any social media site that was tailored specifically to give love to Etsians, it would have to be Pinterest.

Sorry to sound like a used car salesman, but I cover pretty extensively in my "How to Sell on Etsy with Pinterest" guide. (You can check it out at: CraftBizInsider.com/pinterest.)

The key thing I want to reiterate is, if you're an Etsy seller…

YOU NEED TO GET ON PINTEREST!

Etsy is niched towards arts & crafts sellers – and because Pinterest is a quasi-social bookmarking/picture/info-graphic social media site, it opens up the perfect opportunity to showcase your stuff.

Studies have shown that going viral on Pinterest will likely result in a major sales climb.

Now it does take a bit of time and effort to build up your Pinterest platform. Unlike Facebook, you've got to do more than just post a couple times a week to see some worthwhile return.

But if you already use Pinterest, or you've got somebody on your team who can devote some time to Pinterest, then get in the habit of:

- **Pinning a photo from every blog post** you create on Pinterest.

- **Make sure to use keywords** in the title and description of each pin.

- **Do a search on Pinterest to find other people** who might be interested in the keyword associated to your blog post. Then follow them, see if they follow you back and send some more traffic your way.

- **Bonus points: Create a keyword-friendly name** for the pin board that the pin is associated to.

The Google denies it, but I do think sharing your blog posts on Pinterest greatly boosts your content's ability to be found in search engines.

And frankly, the web is getting more and more visual. So ensuring you have a clear footprint in the Pinterest forest will be time well spent.

Blueprint method No.5: Anything Else You Like and Enjoy

But what about YouTube, Google Plus, Tumblr, GoodReads, or message boards or Instagram…?

Yes, yes and yes!

If there's a social network you currently use —
and enjoy spending time with — then by all means
use it to promote your Etsy store.

But there are only so many hours in the day —
and social networks we can scour — and at some
point you've got to say…"Enough!"

**But trust me: Stick with this for a little while
and you'll see amazing things.**

You'll create blog content and find it shared all
around the world. You'll get emails from fans across
the globe — and find new customers in some of the
most random regions of this planet.

Because blogging isn't just words on a page, or a
video or photo embedded in a blog post. It's YOU
sharing your art, exposing your soul. Expressing your
own unique perspective on the world with total
strangers.

And that takes real guts, and real compassion.
(Something that mystifies most non-Etsy folks.)

So, stick with this blogging "thing." It's not an
overnight success, but a slow burn that can lead to a

raging inferno.

Chapter 6 Action Steps:

- **Build a passionate army of Facebook fans.** Then, turn that army, through kick-butt blog content, into leads and customers.

- **Use a scheduling tool, such as HootSuite, to make your Twitter marketing efforts seamless.** Don't forget to include the [TYPE] of media in your tweet, an eye-catching title, and a hashtag (#) that helps your tweet get discovered.

- **Use Social Media Bookmarking sites like StumbleUpon and Technorati to help your blog content get discovered.** You might even find other cool Etsy sellers to network with.

- **Embrace the power of Pinterest.** Share every photo of every blog post you can. Don't forget to optimize your pin titles and descriptions with keywords.

Chapter 7:
Case Studies

"A man without a smiling face must not open a shop."

-Chinese Proverb

It is at this point in the story where we have a peek outside and talk about what I mentioned in the last chapter: other Etsian experiences with these very same methods.

I totally get how friendly advice might seem a little baseless without real-world examples of its effectiveness —so that's why I wanted to include case studies on successful Etsians that have been featured in major crafter-artisan entrepreneur blogs.

One such blog, Handmadeology.com, is not only a fantastic resource for advice and tips on how to rock an Etsy business –but they also regularly post success stories. The point I want you to get from all of this: It can be done. Because it's been done many times before.`

If You List It, They Will (Not) Come…

One of my favorite case studies comes from the owner of Aerides Designs. In a way, she's the classic Etsian, who learned the hard way that simply starting a shop and listing something –doesn't equate to selling anything:

"Once you have a wonderful product, marketing is really more important than anything else – so many wonderful shops list a few amazing items, then weeks later come to the Etsy forums asking why they haven't sold yet.

"You can't 'list it and they will come' – not even seasoned full time sellers. The business aspect, fortunately for me, [is] as attractive as the creative side."

Two interesting pieces of this puzzle really stuck out to me with this particular shop owner:

She mentioned she started her business, because

of her love of the craft. She was already passionate about what she was doing, and only later, did she begin to love the business part of Etsy.

She mentioned you can't just list something on Etsy and expect to get any sales...

For Etsians, this is ESSENTIAL to what I've been talking about! You can't build a living and a fortune from your Etsy store alone —it's just not going to happen. At the end of the day, you've got to go **big** with your online marketing tactics (or simply expect to make meager sales).

A Month In ...And She Already Gets It

Jessica Reiss Photography is an EXCELLENT example of a newbie Etsian (with a baby shop that was only a month old).

But not only is this shop owner aware of the fact that running an Etsy biz is very challenging in the beginning – she was also doing so, with the understanding that she's gotta reach out to social media, be proactive online and not get stuck in the quicksand of thinking that a shop lives and dies on Etsy:

"Having just started Etsy about a month ago, I have realized that I need to market my work extensively. I have made a Facebook page for my work, have joined Twitter and have made a Pinterest account as well.

"Business is hard to get into, especially with no background in it at all, but I am learning as I go- getting advice from others who have been successful and reading online A LOT. Overall, that it's not that easy to sell and it takes time to get yourself out there."

Can I get an AMEN!?

By the way, not only has she recently been featured on several major blogs, but she runs her own website, and markets on Pinterest, Facebook and Twitter. As of this date, it looks like she's doing pretty well for herself.

Etsy Blogging ...To Fairyland

If we're going to talk about branding, marketing and making it big on Etsy through a blog – a great example of this is the owner of Fairyfolk. In an interview from Handmadeology.com, she is true-blooded Etsian —complete with the felt, craftiness, frills… and well… fairies.

Nevertheless, she found out early on, just how POWERFUL running a successful blog can be:

"My blog has worked wonders. The Magic Onions started off as an avenue for me to share our days with my mom and dad, who live many oceans away from us. I wanted them to be involved in our every-day happenings. I was utterly fascinated to find that I had 'unrelated' followers.

"Soon, more people tuned in for our daily dose of family goings-on. Within a few months, I realized that I had a tiger by the tail… people were looking to us for daily inspiration; crafty, nature-inspired, mamma's who are just like me. I found I experienced a genuine pleasure in sharing with them. It's been amazing how I inspire others who, in turn, inspire me to inspire. Aah, it's just a gosh dang circle of love!"

She's now an online craft sensation – and what's more, she's living the dream of influencing lives.

"Aah, it's just a gosh dang circle of love!"…that's what I like to hear.

The Go-Getter: Etsians, This Could Be You.

Tis true, your mileage may vary – but for some, wild and uninhibited success could lay just around the corner. It didn't take Energy Shop's owner long to understand that:

The ability to step outside your comfort zone pays fortunes and earns success.

This shop owner pulled out ALL the stops, hit the ground running… and within months, she went viral. Her story:

"It's the Energy Shop's second anniversary, and I love to write a big post every year to celebrate how far it's come and what I've learned. It started with:

450 Sales on Etsy in the First 3 Months and 1,000 Sales and Counting in Year 1

"As I began to gather together what I've learned in the last two years of business, it became clear that the post was going to be epic.

"Before I knew it, there were seven pages of ideas, marketing strategy and tips that had poured out of me onto the page. As author of the blog, Marketing Creativity, it's no secret that I love the business side of my shop as much as I love making the products I sell."

If there were ever an example that provides an excellent lesson on what success COULD happen – then this would have to be my go-to girl.

However, there's a reason why I wanted to touch on other powerful examples of people who were just starting out and learning the hard lessons.

The secret is: IF WE learn FROM THEM… then, my friend, you're way **ahead** of the curve.

Well, I Hope You Had a Great Time…

I just want to thank you for reading this book, and I sure hope you were able to learn quite a bit. I also hope that from those case studies – you realize… you can TOTALLY do this.

Being an Etsy high-seller sensation is completely within your reach. All you need to do is extend your arms and white-knuckle grasp it with both hands.

Though, there is one more thing I'd like to impress upon you…

Never stop learning. I believe that's a part of the unique luster of being an Etsian: We're always creating, always seeking what moves us, always becoming more independent... and we're constantly evolving.

This eBook should be more than enough to get your marketing efforts off the ground and aiming for the stars – but these tactics are in a constant state of evolution.

Be sure to keep up your research and never stop trying to find new, faster, easier, more effective ways to cultivate your online herb garden patch.

A Special FREE Gift for You!

If you'd like FREE instant access to my special report "Top 10 Marketing Tools Every Etsy Seller Should Use" then head over to **CraftBizInsider.com/Free**.

(What else you gonna do? Watch another "Twilight" movie?!)

Made in the USA
Columbia, SC
12 March 2021